IMAGES OF ENGLAND

Around Tring

Gilbert Grace & Son in Western Road, later renamed the High Street. In the 1880s it had been further down, at 34 High Street, before that in Akeman Street, and in the 1870s Sebastian Grace had promises near the old Market House, demolished in 1900, that stood in the front of the church. It was established in 1750, possibly in Frogmore Street. Graces were the manufacturers of many of the beautiful wrought iron gates seen in the early photographs. They also did a lot of work for the Rothschilds in the construction of the Museum, and are still a successful traditional ironmongers. Mrs Emma Grace, the great-grandmother of the present Gilbert Grace, can be seen in this photograph

IMAGES OF ENGLAND

Around Tring

Mike Bass & Jill Fowler

NONSUCH

First published 1996
This new pocket edition 2006
Images unchanged from first edition

Nonsuch Publishing Limited
The Mill, Brimscombe Port,
Stroud, Gloucestershire, GL5 2QG
www.nonsuch-publishing.com

Nonsuch Publishing is an imprint of Tempus Publishing Group

British Library Cataloguing in Publication Data.
A catalogue record for this book is available from the British Library.

ISBN 1-84588-327-6

Typesetting and origination by Nonsuch Publishing Limited
Printed in Great Britain by Oaklands Book Services Limited

Contents

Acknowledgements

Wendy Austin: Hugh and Margaret Bass: Jean Bradding: Bert Brooks
Connie Carter: Cholesbury-cum-St Leonards History Society
George Christopher: George Cobby: John and Pam Cockerill: Peter Cook Mick
Higgins: Shirley Fisher: Frank Gower: Pat Gower
Peter and Thelma Gower: Bob Grace: Gilbert and Julie Grace: Nora Grace Phil
and Gary Harrop: Jeff Hawkins: Stephen Hearn
Hedley and Dulcie Hopcroft: the late Bob Hummer: Audrey Kempster
David Kempster: Ron Kitchener: Florence and Gordon McAndrew
Pat Moss-Carlsson: Doreen Moy: Mrs Nurden: George and Dorothy Prentice
Arthur Reed: Don and Ann Reed: Janet and Simon Rigby: John Rotheroe Ralph
Seymour: Doug Sinclair: Peggy Slemeck: Jeannie and Frank Standen Mrs Roland
Stevens: Eirlys Thomas
Tring and District Local History and Museum Society: 1st Tring Scout Group
Tring Park Cricket Club: Philip Watts: Ron Wheeler.

Introduction

Tring is first mentioned in the Anglo-Saxon Record of AD 571, several centuries before nearby larger towns. In the Domesday book, compiled in 1086 on the instruction of William the Conqueror, it was called Treunge or Tredunga. By the thirteenth century one of the names referring to the town was Trehanger, a name given to a ladies social club in Tring seven centuries later. The town's position where the ancient Icknield Way crossed the Roman road, Akeman Street, ensured opportunities for local merchants to trade, and, with the coming of the Grand Junction Canal and the London to Birmingham Railway Company early in the nineteenth century, Tring soon became a prosperous and thriving market town.

Tring is said to have had a parish church for more than 700 years, but little, if anything, is left of the first building on the site, which probably predates the Norman Conquest. Some of the interesting features in the church date back to the fifteenth century, such as the original arches and the stone corbels between them, but there have been a lot of alterations and rebuilding since then. The church contains six bells, dating from 1624 to 1882, when a major restoration was completed. Other denominations are also well represented in Tring, and in the surrounding villages most of the churches date in part back to the twelfth or thirteenth century, an exception being St Cross, Wilstone, completed in 1877.

The arrival of Nathaniel Rothschild, of the famous banking family, to Tring Park in 1872 made a considerable impact on the people of Tring. He and Lady Rothschild took a benevolent interest in the town and employed local people in the various projects in which they were involved. It was said that if an unemployed local person approached Lord Rothschild's agent he would be found a position somewhere on the estate. Nathan's son, Walter, founded the Tring Museum which was opened to the public in 1892. Today the magnificent displays of birds, animals and insects are part of the British Museum and attract thousands of visitors a year.

A lot of older buildings in Tring have disappeared, due in the early days to the Rothschilds' clearance for their own projects, and due later to council redevelopment. However much remains that can still be recognised when compared with Victorian and Edwardian photographs, and descendants of many of the old families still live in Tring. The town is still a pleasant place in which to live, there are no multi-story car parks, no green glass skyscrapers and no giant supermarkets, though an application for one of the latter has been put forward recently. The Tring by-pass, opened in 1975, has relieved the traffic congestion in the centre of the town to some extent, but parking is still a problem, especially in the older parts where the houses were built some time before the invention of the motor car.

We have tried to gather together a collection of photographs that reflects the character of Tring and shows how the people lived, worked and enjoyed themselves. The descriptions of the photographs have been written with the help of many of the older citizens of the town, often remembering people and events dating back over fifty years. We thank them all and hope we have recorded the facts correctly. If you feel you can add anything more to the story of Tring in the past we would be very pleased to hear from you.

One

Around the Town

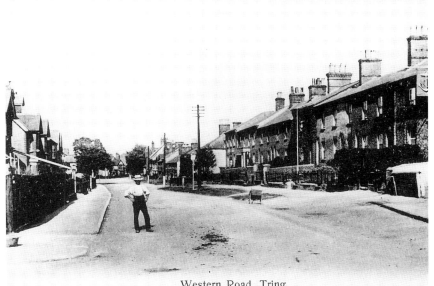

Western Road, Tring.

Western Road in around 1914 viewed from the Chapel Street–Miswell Lane crossroads. The Anchor public house is much the same today, as are the cottages beyond it. Mr Rolfe's house and the Western Hall in the centre of the photograph have now been demolished to make way for the new houses in Stanley Gardens.

Above and below: Two photographs taken early in the twentieth century of Western Road. Above, between the two blocks of houses (see page 37) was Mr Hobbs stonemasons yard. Next to the last block is now a more modern detached house and next to that used to be the Regal Cinema, built in 1936. The Regal was demolished in 1960 and ten flats built on the site, named Regal Court. The view below has changed little.

The Upper High Street in the 1880s, then called Western Road. After Prouse's, the saddlers, can be seen the Post Office but beyond that more shops have yet to be built. On the right is Ivy Cottage, Miss Wilson's Dame School, and beyond that can be seen the National School.

Post office?

Tring High Street c. 1910. A Whitsun procession has paraded through the town and is returning to the school before going to the Park for a picnic. These processions continued until well into the century.

Tring High Street c. 1904 at the Frogmore Street–Akeman Street crossroads. The Market House is on the right but the police station has yet to be built next to it. Mr William Bayman Humphrey of Park Road stands at the front. He looks a dignified gentleman and for many years represented the Imperial Fire Insurance Company. A retired builder, Mr Humphrey died on 21 May 1920 and was buried on his ninety-fourth birthday.

The corner of Akeman Street and the High Street in the 1890s, from the crossroads upwards. The house is that of Mr Mead, the butcher, and beyond is his shop and slaughterhouse. The buildings stood well out into the street and made the main road very narrow at this point. In the distance the National School building can just be seen.

Market House, Tring

The Market House on the corner of Akeman Street. It was built at the turn of the twentieth century on the site of Mr Mead's premises, replacing the old Market House in front of the church. It was opened in 1901, designed by Lord Rothschild's architect, William Huckvale, and paid for by local subscription as a memorial to Queen Victoria's Diamond Jubilee.

The Market House in the 1970s, the ground floor was enclosed around 1910. It was later used to house the fire engine and the fire siren was in the bell tower on the roof. The larger size of modern fire engines necessitated the move to a purpose-built fire station in Brook Street. The police station can be seen just beyond the Market House.

The High Street in the 1930s. On the left is Arthur Gates, stationers, now The Motorists Centre. In the distance De Fraines, also a stationers, was on the corner just this side of the Rose and Crown Hotel. The imposing building with the pillars is the Nat West Bank, which is this side of the Midland Bank. Adjacent to it are the premises that housed the doctor's surgery until a purpose-built surgery was recently opened in Western Road. Lovibonds, the wine merchant, was still trading well within living memory, and Smith's Chemist remains, renamed Lloyds.

The High Street in the 1890s. In the far distance the public house, The Green Man can just be seen. This side of it the tall ivy-covered building is the premises of Ebenezer Charles Bird, booksellers, stationers and printers. It was later demolished by the Rothschilds and replaced by the mock-Tudor house built for their estate accountant. At this time the old Rose and Crown was level with the other shops which have been rebuilt early in the twentieth century. On the left we see the premises of Brown & Foulkes, now Brown & Merry estate agents, but the shops and old Market House beyond were part of the clearance to open up the view to the church.

Tring High Street c. 1900. John Bly Senior opened his shop at 22 High Street in the early 1890s, selling china and furniture, the forerunner of the well known antique business. They later moved to 50 High Street, and the Midland Bank was built on the site of this and the butchers shop next door. On the left one of Tring's oldest inns, The Bell can just be seen.

The High Street around 1960 after Sanders, the fruiterers, had closed. Clements the jewellers, watch and clockmakers, was still open. Both were demolished to make the entrance to the Dolphin Square shopping precinct.

Tring High Street in the early 1880s. This scene depicts a parade of the Society of Oddfellows and the Tring Band surrounded by locals. Butchers Bank, now the Nat-West is on the left, and in the far distance is Ivy Cottage. At this time there were few other buildings on that part of the High Street.

The High Street in the 1880s, with Butchers Bank on the left. Just beyond, Mr William Johnson stands outside his butchers shop where he lived with his wife Sarah, their two sons and four daughters. Next door Mr Henry Johnson kept the fishmongers shop, and the large arch past the surgery is the entrance to Tring Brewery, occupied by John Brown. On the right is the Bell Inn and Sharman's clothes shop.

Miss Butcher taught wine at Sunday school

The High Street in 1900, as the old Market House was being knocked down. It was demolished because the people of Tring wanted to build a new Market House to commemorate Queen Victoria's Diamond Jubilee. Old records tell of a Market House in 1650 with a corn loft over it. A description of 1819 said it was 'a mean edifice on wooden pillars having a pillory and cage underneath'. Any person found wandering the streets of Tring who was the worse for drink could end up spending the night locked in the cage. The area up to the Brown & Merry building was cleared and was left open so all could enjoy the view of the church.

Tring High Street in the 1970s. The view of the church as it has been seen from the Rose and Crown forecourt after both the old Market House and Rose and Crown had been demolished. It remained a car park until the High Street improvements in 1991, which then gave an even better view of the church.

The Lower High Street on market day in the 1890s. The Rothschilds moved the livestock market from this High Street site, where it had been held for many centuries, down to a new purpose-built market in Brook Street. The general market stayed on this roadside location until the 1970s.

Market day in the 1970s. As in the previous picture the market is still on the pavement in the Lower High Street. When the new car park was built on the grassed area behind these stalls, the Friday market was held there as it is today.

The far end of the High Street with Station Road in the distance. The decorations are for the visit of the Prince of Wales, later King Edward VII, in 1897, the year of Queen Victoria's Diamond Jubilee. Mr Woodman stands outside his Green Man Inn.

The London Road, Brook Street end of Tring with another procession, in the thirties, turning to march back through the town. The Unity Hall is on the left, and on the hill can be seen the rectory, later demolished, and now there are modern houses on the site.

Tring Market, Brook Street. The Market was built by the Rothschilds in the 1880s. There had been a livestock market in Tring since the thirteenth century but before it moved to Brook Street it would have been held in the High Street, called 'Market Street'. The business was run for many years by Messrs W. Brown & Co, and more recently by Brown & Merry, the estate agents and auctioneers. Although it retains the name, it is now owned by Mr Stephen Hearn. The livestock sales have been phased out and now the buildings are the venue for general goods and fine art sales.

Christchurch Road in the 1960s when it was still a no through road. In the distance can be seen Osmington School, formerly Okeford House, and the road did not go far beyond that point. The detached houses were just being built along each side of the road, and the entrance to Goldfield Road is on the left.

Henry Street. The small streets of Tring were seldom photographed unless an interesting event was taking place, as here, on Jubilee Day in May 1935. The couple at the front are Emily and Alfred Crockett who lived at No. 30. Mr Crockett had been a carrier all his working life and is remembered driving the railway horse and cart. In the 1891 census Emily and Alfred were living at No. 30, and were aged twenty-two and twenty-four respectively. The tall figure standing in the road on the left is Jack Smith.

Looking up Chapel Street in the 1960s. The cottages remain mostly unchanged but the barn and the corner premises, formerly a builders yard owned by the Finchers and later by Potter Bros. plumbers and decorators, have been replaced by the new doctors surgery. In the distance can be seen St Marthas church and the large tree that became a victim of the gales some years later.

King Street in the 1970s, with the Kings Arms in the distance. Behind the trees was the big house, The Furlong, built by the Revd Arthur Frederick Pope in the middle of the nineteenth century. More recently it was used as the Convents Junior School but was demolished in the late 1980s and replaced by flats and gardens, also called The Furlong. This part of King Street was built on land known as Gravelly Furlong and the house just visible beyond the trees, now called Gravelly House, was originally Gravelly Infants School.

Park Road early in the nineteenth century, showing the Museum, in the background, and the Louisa Cottages on the left. The turning to the left is Akeman Street, ahead is Park Street and to the right is the Chesham Road. These buildings are still much the same today.

Looking down Akeman Street, from Park Road, in the 1870s. The men on the left are in front of The Swan public house while the lady in the crinoline is standing by the premises of Mr Evans the silk weaver, later Rodwell's brewery. In the distance is the Royal Oak, one of five public houses in Akeman Street. On the right, where the Rothschild Museum will soon be built, is the barn of Mr Fincher's Town Farm.

Closed shops and cottages on the Akeman Street–Albert Street corner just before they were demolished to make way for the new buildings of the William Batey electronics business, already in Akeman Street. In 1882 the corner building was occupied by Joseph Budd, a 'Marine Store Dealer' and later, in 1910, Ebenezer Prentice was running the business.

Akeman Street contains some of the oldest buildings in Tring. On the right is Graces Mill, now called Graces Maltings and parts of this building go back to medieval times. Opposite the Mill was a bakers run by Edward Grace and his wife Jane which later became Warriors bakery shop. Further down is the Harrow public house which was pulled down in the late 1950s. The area behind is still called Harrow Yard. The building at the end of the street is Mr Mead's house which was knocked down when the Market House was built.

Cato's weaving shop in Park Road in the 1890s. There were several weaving shops in Tring, making rough canvas for items like horses nosebags through to fine canvas used for embroidery. Cato's started originally in Tabernacle Yard in Akeman Street but George Cato later ran his business at 12 Charles Street. The premises in Park Road employed a lot of young boys who were 'half-timers' from school. The building was later demolished as part of Lord Rothschild's clearance of the south side of Park Road. The Chapel Street–King Street junction can just be seen in the distance.

An early photograph of Parsonage Place. In the 1890s James Darvill and his wife Rachel lived in Parsonage Place Farm with their four nephews and nieces. Although this area has been altered over the years, many of the buildings still exist as modernised private dwellings.

A view of Parsonage Place in the 1970s. The large ancient barn at the back has sadly been severely damaged after a nearby shed was set alight and the fire spread to the barn. The building just this side of it can be seen on the left-hand side of the photograph above. In the 1890s some eight families lived in Parsonage Place including shoe makers, plumbers and decorators, straw plaiters and carpenters. The cottages have now been renovated and are again occupied.

Above: Frogmore Street photographed in 1971. In the 1890s Johnson's fish shop was still a private house and part of Frogmore Street. Hy Johnson, fishmonger, first appears in Kellys Directory in 1899. It is now No. 1 Parsonage Place, and has been a restaurant for some years. In the far distance is Barnetts the bakers which, in the 1880s, was run by Ann Putman, and in the 1930s by Edwin Burch. Many of the buildings on the right have now been demolished and replaced by the Dolphin Square shopping centre. The Dolphin Inn used to stand in the space between the buildings on the right in this photograph.

New Mill in the 1930s. Brook Street stretches into the distance on its way to Tring. The public house on the left is The Pheasant, now refurbished and renamed The New Mill.

Above: Wingrave Road *c.* 1930. Benjamin Saunders Gower ran the post office and store, seen on the right, which is now a hairdressers. The other cottages have changed little, although The Queens Arms, in the distance, has gone.

Opposite below: Frogmore Street photographed in the early 1970s. The building on the far right is Barnetts the bakers. The low building next to it still stands but the other two have since been demolished. In 1891 the central building was the premises of Alfred Chapman, pawnbroker, and to the left lived the Revd Charles Pearce, Baptist minister. This is now the entrance to the Frogmore Street car park.

Grove Road, leading to New Mill. Marshcroft Lane leads off to the right.

Houses in Grove Road, in the 1950s which look much the same today.

A row of houses in Marshcroft Lane, off Grove Road, leading to Park Hill Farm.

A closer view of the last pair of houses, showing the handsome windows and tile-hung walls of these Pendley Estate houses.

Plans for the Grand Junction Canal were drawn up in 1791, the chief engineer being William Jessop. Work was started in 1793 and since all the work was done by hand, it took 6,000 people around four years to complete it, at the cost of about a million pounds. The canal, now called the Grand Union, saw considerable trade for almost two centuries, the last regular commercial traffic being in the 1980s. Pleasure boats and fisherman are still a regular feature of the canal and the miles of towpaths attract walkers.

Goldfield Mill at the top of Miswell Lane. The mill was built in 1840 by Mr Grover, formerly in partnership with the Mead family, who had their business at New Mill. Mr Grover had a disagreement with Mr Mead and built his own mill by the Icknield Way. The mill, without its sails, is now a private house.

The Oddy Hill goes up from Tring to Wigginton. The word 'oddy' was said to represent a type of Hertfordshire snail but a preferred version was that it meant a triangular headland, a shape it makes with the other road, the Twist. The Rothschild's summer house can be seen, in good condition, early in the twentieth century. It was lived in during the last war by the actress, Peggy Ashcroft, but much has now sadly crumbled. What remains is being repaired and preserved.

WEST LEITH NEAR TRING

The countryside along Duckmore Lane. This pair of cottages still stands at the fork. The left road leads to West Leith Farm and Stubbins Wood and straight on to Lord Rothschild's stud farm, Terriers End and Dancers End.

A view from the Oddy Hill. Taken around 1930, shows the Ivinghoe Beacon in the distance and, has changed little over the years.

The Upper Icknield Way, the ancient route that runs along the north side of the town, with the Ivinghoe Beacon in the background. This road to Dunstable and Whipsnade Zoo has also changed little over the years, though it is no longer suitable for cattle to walk along.

Above left: Evans Spring, Hastoe Lane. Mrs Fulks sitting on the stile.

Above right: The Holloway, a very ancient track, goes up through Stubbins Wood from West Leith to Hastoe.

Above left: Stubbins Wood started above Home Farm and ascended to Hastoe and along, as Pavis Wood, towards Paynes End. It was approached by a public footpath from Park Road, now diverted to Hastoe Lane, due to the building of the Tring bypass.

Above right: A view near Tring, the road to Dancers End. The house on the left was Gillinghams where sausage skins were made – it is said that, if the wind was in the wrong direction, the smell was awful.

An aerial view of Tring in the late 1960s. The museum can be seen in the top right hand corner. In the bottom right hand corner are the first buildings of Bishop Wood School but the old High Street School and the masters house are still there too. On the left, the market car park has not yet been built and the allotments to the left of the Black Horse pub are still there.

Moving in closer we can see the top of the Rose and Crown and the NatWest and Midland Banks in the High Street. The Dolphin Square shopping precinct has yet to be built but the demolition of the area east of the church has started and only part of Church Lane and Westwood Lane remain.

Two

Shops and Businesses

Benjamin Saunders Gower ran the post office and general store, early in the twentieth century, in New Mill and later set up a grocers and fruiterers shop in Western Road. This view, taken in the early 1950s, also shows Sketchley cleaners, now in the High Street, and Charles Atkin, baker.

KINGHAM BROS., WESTERN ROAD, TRING.

Benjamin Kingham founded his cycle shop in the last decade of the nineteenth century, when cycling was in its pioneer days. His son, Reginald, can be seen in the photograph. When his wife died, Benjamin married for a second time, to Ellen Hopcroft, in 1904, and their son, Jack, later took over the business and ran it until he retired in 1971. Ellen lived to be Tring's first centenarian since the turn of the twentieth century and died in 1967 at the age of 101. In the photograph are: Horace Hedley Hopcroft, Benjamin Kingham, Reginald Kingham and an employee, thought to be Frank Batchelor.

Byatts came from there. ✗

Young Hedley Hopcroft tries out a motor bicycle from Kinghams Cycle Stores. The lane runs behind the shop in Western Road and the houses on the right hand side are one of four pairs of older houses in Goldfield Road.

John Gower and Son's waggon, photographed in 1910 at the junction of Brook Street and London Road. The Robin Hood can be seen on the left. The business was founded in 1876 and in the early 1900s was trading from premises in Queen Street and Western Road, dealing in coal, coke, wood and furniture removals. Before the First World War, Gowers had sixteen horses but several of them were taken for war work. Travelling to Manchester or Leeds to make deliveries by rail the horses would be put in a horse box on the train and the pantechnicon on rolling stock.

James Hobbs the stonemasons in Western Road. The business was previously at Bottle Cross at the end of Park Road opposite the Britannia public house but was cleared away in the late 1880s. They then moved to Western Road and James Hobbs Senior can be seen there in this photograph taken around 1910. In 1891 forty-four-year-old James Snr, a widower, was living here with his son, also James, aged nineteen. James Jnr had two daughters, Mary and Fanny, and a son, Arthur.

Above: Tring High Street, then called Western Road, in the early 1900s. On the right is Frederick Johnson's watchmakers shop. The 1891 census records him living there with his wife, Mary, and sixteen-year-old assistant Amos Gurney. In the shop next door Robert William Allison was a corn merchant and the business was still being run by his wife, Lucy, in the late 1930s. The sign above Frederick Waldock's bakers and confectioners can still be seen today as it was uncovered by the present proprietors, Jon Hall Interiors. Further down can be seen the Gazette Office and Cosier and Sons, high-class tailors who moved to No. 35 High Street in the late 1930s. The man with the wheelbarrow is Joe 'Chops' and he is delivering coal.

Brackets come from there ✗

Opposite below: As early as 1899 Kelly's listed Cash & Co., boot manufacturers in the Western Road. They were still there in 1937 but by then the road had been renamed, and they were now at No. 76 High Street. In this earlier photograph of around 1914 we see Mr Harlow standing outside the shop with his assistant Albert Prentice. The premises later became Turners shoe shop and more recently an estate agents. The library is now to the left.

Right: Mr Edgar Bagnall stands in the doorway of his watchmaker and jewellers shop at 71 High Street. Edgar previously had a shop at 62 Akeman Street and around 1930 he moved up to the High Street or Western Road as it was called then. The shop was formerly the premises of Harry & Herbert Foskett, high-class boot and shoe manufacturers. This photograph was taken by the present proprietor, Mr Brian Planton, when he took over the shop on Mr Bagnall's retirement in 1964.

Below: The High Street Crossroads. Edward James Stevens cycle shop started in the early days of cycling and sold 'Yusemee' cycles which were made up on the premises. The shop was divided, with the cycle parts on one side and musical instruments and sheet music on the other; later, records and radios were introduced. This shop is now Arthur Starling's shoe shop but there is still a small department selling cycle parts. The shop on the corner, E. Gates and Son, sold tobacco, sweets, stationery and fancy goods. During the First World War it was run by Mrs Gates, and later by Arthur Gates, who also had a hairdressing business opposite at No.25a.

Left: Mr George E. Goddard, a former railway inspector, purchased the confectionery and newsagents business at No.29 High Street, now The Wool Shop, in 1913, for £130. In 1925, his nephew, George William Goddard, bought the shop next door, No.28, and the business was transferred there in 1927. This photograph, taken in 1937, shows George William Goddard standing in the doorway of No.28.

Below: Nos 31 and 32 High Street, here the premises of Robert Harrison & Sons. From the nineteenth century until the 1930s it was called Manchester House and was home to Richard Greening's tailors, drapers and clothiers business. Here, Tring people are queuing with their children to meet Father Christmas in the 1960s. The shop was later occupied by Charles Philips and Tescos, all self-service grocers, and now, considerably modernised, is the premises of the Woolwich.

Right: Clements jewellers, watch and clockmakers. The Clement business started as far back as 1773 and stayed at 33 High Street until it closed down in the 1960s. No other firm in Tring had occupied the same premises for so long. The business has always serviced and repaired the clock mechanism in the parish church. In 1891 John Tripp Clement was the clock and watchmaker. A widower, he lived there with his children, two sons and five daughters, one of the sons being John Lovett, then eleven years of age.

Below: Mr John Lovett Clement at his workbench behind his High Street shop. Mr Clement was an accomplished musician and as a young man he was the organist at the High Street Free Church. He was also a keen historian and his records of the past provide valuable information to those researching Tring's history. He was unmarried and when he retired, the business closed. He died in 1964.

Above: In the 1890s No.35 High Street was the premises of the International Tea Co. and around 1900 they moved to a shop next to Graces in Western Road, with Mr George Simpson as manager. This photograph shows William James Green, motor engineer and cycle maker, at No.35 High Street in around 1908. The sign tells us that they also had works in Harrow Yard, Akeman Street. Later the property was divided into two shops, and in the 1930s was occupied by Cosier & Sons, tailors, and The London Meat Co. Ltd. The shop is now a travel agency.

Wheeler Brothers, towards the lower end of the High Street, in the premises previously held by Ernest Kelsall Fulks drapers. Sidney Wheeler came from London in 1920, when this photograph was taken, and set up a drapery and men's outfitters business in partnership with his brother. Later his son, Ron, ran the shop until his retirement. There are now two businesses here, an estate agents and an opticians.

Right: Mr Thomas Glover and his staff outside his shop at No.19 High Street. Records show that as early as 1851 one Thomas Glover, aged twenty-eight, and Joseph Gates, aged thirty-three, carried on a grocery business there, and it continued until well into the next century. Many Tring people still remember shopping at Glovers. The building is now a wine shop and also houses Tring's post office

Opposite below: On the other side of the High Street, next to the old Tring Brewery arch, we have Sallery and Son, butchers. The business was in Akeman Street in 1882, at No.20, and in the early part of the twentieth century it was at 28 High Street, but a few years later it moved over the road to No.24. Three generations of the Sallery family had this butchers business, the last being Mr Reg Sallery who retired in around 1966. He was Tring's fire chief for ten years and a member of the fire brigade for twenty-one years. The butcher standing in the doorway is Derek Pike.

Harry Johnson, fishmonger, Frogmore Street, now No.1 Parsonage Place. Mr Johnson is in the doorway of his shop. He moved there in the late 1890s from No.22 High Street. Much later in the century the business was run by William Keele, Mr Johnson's son in law. After Parsonage Place was redeveloped the shop then became a restaurant called 'Foxys', recently renamed 'Tringfellows'.

I remember this ✗

Mr George Sayer stands in the doorway of his barbers shop at No.12 Akeman Street. In the nineteenth century it had been occupied by Mrs Ellen Hill, a dressmaker. Records show that George was in business there in 1917 and stayed until the mid thirties; he was a keen musician and was bandmaster of the Salvation Army band. His son, Arthur, continued the business in premises a few doors away at No.9 Akeman Street. In 1937 his old shop was taken over by Ernest Childs, a boot and shoe repairer and some years later became a fish and chip shop.

Reed Photography at No.13 Akeman Street in the 1950s. The shop has previously been a stationers, a fish shop, and a restaurant attached to the fish and chip shop when it was at No.12 next door. Soon after this photograph was taken, Don Reed took over the business on his own and expanded into the premises on the right, later opening shops in Chesham, Aylesbury and Banbury. The Tring branch closed in 1985 when the area was redeveloped and is now private houses. Don Reed retired from the photographic retail trade some years ago

Graces Mill, Akeman Street in the 1970s. It was a malting from medieval times until after the First World War. It continued as a corn mill for about another fifty years, run by Frank Grace and later by his sons Thomas and Robert. Tom and Bob were well known for their lantern slide shows of Old Tring, and Bob Grace still does them, but now with his niece Nuala. In the 1980s the mill was bought up by property developers who transformed the whole area into private dwellings, retaining only some of the original character of this historic building.

Above and below: The interior of Grace's flour mill when it was still in use. The lower photograph shows the mill grinding the corn. The engine used to drive the mill can now be seen at the Pitstone Green Farm Museum.

Mead's flour mill at New Mill around 1900. The 1851 census tells us that William Mead, farmer and mill employer, was at Tring Wharf and was employing twenty workers. The windmill was demolished early in the twentieth century.

Tring Dockyard and boat builders at New Mill. It was first owned by the Mead family who employed John Bushell to build and repair the canal boats which brought grain to their flour mill from the London docks and took back flour. From around 1875 his son Joseph developed the boatyard into a separate business, taking over from Meads in 1912, when Joseph's sons, Charlie and Joseph, were running it. The yard closed when they retired in 1952.

Three

At Work

Laying sewers in Langdon Street. Langdon Street from the Western Road end did not have much to inspire the photographer in the early part of the twentieth century. Cyril Howlett took this picture and it was produced as a postcard. The sewers, taken for granted these days, must have greatly improved the lives of local people.

The blacksmith's forge at No.51 High Street where Thomas Goodson and his son were the blacksmiths. In the next century George Stratford and Eric Reed were among the farriers who shod horses there.

The young man in the blacksmith's shop is Lionel Higby, then aged about seventeen. He was an employee of local farmer Mr Kingsley and had probably taken one of the horses to be shod.

Tring blacksmith, Eric Reed, with a heavy horse in the High Street forge. Born in 1884, and about sixty years old in this picture, Mr Reed cared for the feet of the zebras that Lord Rothschild trained to pull a pony trap. He served in Italy during the First World War as an armourer, repairing guns and shoeing horses.

A horse being shod at Grove c. 1910. Albert Christopher is the blacksmith and holding the shire horse is Joe Croft who was the groom for Sir Gromer-Berry of Pendley Stock Farms. Mr Christopher lived in one of the West Leith cottages with his wife, Ann. She presented him with six sons, one of whom, Albert Christopher jnr, later worked as a chauffeur for Lord Rothschild.

Above: Workers on Mr Kingsley's farm stop for a tea break. Left hand group: Jimmy Croft, Bert Flitney, Mr Seabrook. Centre: Len Fowler. Right hand group: -?-, Mr Kingsley, Lionel Higby (with dog).

Above: A rest while working on the road near Wilstone. The driver is unknown. In front are: Bill Dover, Harry Cartwright, Teddy Crockett, Eric Cartwright, Jack Oakley (road foreman), Harold Edwards, Bob James.

Right: Estate workers pose in front of the huge bonfire built on the downs to celebrate the Coronation of King George V in 1911. It was constructed with great care, with the centre hollow so that it could be lit from the inside and would blaze for a considerable time.

Opposite below: Workers and local people by the remains of one of Tring's windmills. The mill, used by Meads flour mills, was by the canal at New Mill and was knocked down early in the twentieth century. The man at the top is George Hall, who worked for Bushell Bros.

Left: Fireman tackling a fire at Mr Bob Grace's mill in Akeman Street in 1965. The fire, said to be caused by a grain dryer, destroyed the large grain store and drying machinery. Luckily it was prevented from spreading to the historic mill; now known as Graces Maltings. The central figure is Mr Grace.

Below: This railway accident at Tring Station on 1 June 1908 was caused by wrongly set points. Twenty-seven coal trucks, that had come from Nuneaton, should have gone into a siding but went instead into the coal yard, crashing into about eighteen waggons which were already there. A seventeen-year-old boy named Higby, from Harrow Yard in Akeman Street, was crushed and killed instantly. Another lad named Butler was injured and was said by Dr. C. O'Keefe who attended the accident, to be suffering from shock. Also soon to arrive on the scene was Police Sergeant Baldock, from Tring, in response to a telegraph message from the station master. In the photograph the boy holding the shovel is Sydney Gower.

Four

Freetime

Some well-known Tring ladies photographed at a tea party at the vicarage. The group includes the two Miss Hobbs, whose family had the stonemason's yard. Also visible is baby Nora Dell, who later, as Mrs Nora Grace became well known in the town for her unstinting work with the Tring Red Cross, for which she was awarded the MBE. Back row, left to right: Miss Baines, Florrie Gomm, Mabel Fickin, Nancy Reeve, Florence Harding, Mary Hobbs, Mrs Morrison, Elsie Barber, Miss Elliman, Alice Dye, Bess Newcon. Middle row: Alice Waterton, Gwen Waterton, Mrs Rance and son, Annie Collier, Mrs Dell and daughter Nora, Mrs Randall and daughter Florence, Miss Primett, -?-, Mrs Collins, Stan Fletcher, Mrs Fletcher. Front row: Doris Gomm, Fanny Hobbs, Edie Jennings, -?-, Cis Howlett, Ivy Lee, Kath Collins, Dorothy Newcon.

Tring YMCA Gymnast Team. Back row: Sid Lovell M, Sid Horn, Arthur Church, ? Swaby (Aldbury), Frank Bly, -?-, -?-, -?-, Bill Budd, -?-. Third row: 'Decko' Budd, ? Gomm, John Prentice. Second row: Jack Lines, Stan Minall, Mac Rush, ? Wright, -?-, ? Budd, Gillie Rance. Front row: Joe Lovell, ? Poulton, Jack Kingham, ? Collins, -?-, ? Bligh, Bobbie Bell.

In June 1914 the YMCA team gave a gymnastic display to raise funds for the local hospitals. The ground is that of the Tring Park Cricket Club and Station Road can be seen in the background.

Mr Frederick Reeve with his group of bell ringers outside Tring church. Back row: -?-, Harry Bull, Visiting ringer, Chris Badrick, Visiting ringer, ? Cherry?, Harold Brackley, Jesse Puplett, Harry Jones, Front row: -?-, Frederick Reeve, Nathan Brackley. Mr Frederick James Reeve was born in Tring in 1873. He was an enthusiastic bell-ringer for most of his life and travelled all over England visiting other churches and joining their teams ringing different bells. He was also a member of Tring Fire Brigade, which he joined in 1912.

Akeman Street Baptist church outing to the Wembley Exhibition of 1924. The charabanc was supplied by Mr Prentice from Western Road. Back row: (standing and sitting) Dorothy Wright, Frank Bly, -?-, Rose West, Miss Ginny West, Miss Osbourne, Miss Fincher, John 'Tommy' Chapman, Cissie Chapman, Front row: Mr Hedges, Harold Howlett, Phyllis Howlett, Miss King, Alice Smith, Mrs Smith, Mr Fincher, Miss Olive Foskett, Mrs Fincher, (small boy) Bobby Fincher, Nellie Reeve, -?-, -?-, Daisy Hedges, Lily Hedges, Miss Hedges. In front: (boy) Alfred Wright, Mr Sidney Garrad (pastor of chapel), Driver -?-.

A Sunday School group early in the twentieth century walking up Langdon Street on their way to Tring park, where they would play games and enjoy a picnic. These houses look much the same today. The turning into Charles Street on the left can just be seen in the distance, with the Co-operative Stores, butchers and bakery on the corner, now converted into private dwellings. Just this side can be seen the railings of the Methodist Church, now demolished and replaced by a pair of semi-detached houses.

A coach outing for members of New Mill Baptist Church in the 1930s. The lady on the left hand side in the front row is Mrs Welling, whose husband was a member of the Tring Fire Brigade for many years. Just beyond her on the back row the hatless man is Mr Dando, the Baptist minister and further along the line are Mr and Mrs Randall, Charlie Wilkins, Mrs Welling and Albert Christopher.

Tring YMCA floats in Tring Park for the Jubilee Day Celebrations in 1935. The man in the dark fez on the left hand float is 'Nobby' Rance, well known in Tring as he was the manager of the Charles Street Co-op. The man in the Indian costume is Frank Bly. On the other float are: Roland Rance, George Christopher, Fred Waterton, Wally Rance, Bert Wright, and 'Knock' Higby with the dog. Standing by the float are Frank Johnson and Harold Brackley. Standing by the horse is Billy Mills.

Another YMCA float with: Len Lovegrove (Australian), Stanley Fletcher (Britannia), Archie Fulks (John Bull), Bert Wright and Stanley Wright (each side of John Bull). The man holding the horse is Marsworth-born, Dennis Johnson.

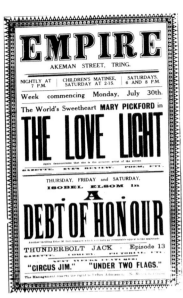

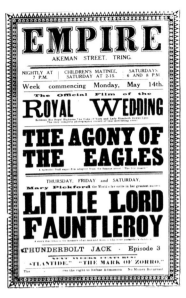

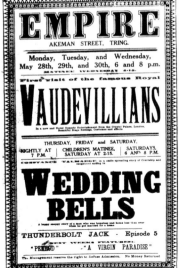

This page: Posters for films shown at the Empire Picture Palace Theatre in Akeman Street in the early 1920s. The Empire opened in 1916 only a few days before the rival Gem in Western Road. The Gem only survived for a few years and the Empire, renamed the Gaiety in 1932, remained the only cinema until the Regal was opened in Western Road in 1936. This had a severe effect and the Gaiety's popularity waned, but it did not close until war broke out in 1939. The building is still there, used as business premises.

Opposite above: The site of the first Gem cinema in the lower High Street, where Tring's first cinema was opened in 1912. The Unity Hall was above the Tring Co-op. It held 300 people and, with a 19-foot-deep stage, was often used for plays. Alterations were made and it was turned into the Gem picture hall, with P.J. Darvell the licensee. He later built a new Gem cinema in Western Road, but this did not survive for long, as at the same time the Empire was being built in Akeman Street, and the Gem closed in the early 1920s. These premises, still marked Unity Hall on the doorway, are now the Frances Elizabeth Crystal Rooms, used for banquets and wedding receptions.

Below: The Regal cinema opened on 10 September 1936. It did very good business during the Second Wold War, the population of Tring being swelled by evacuees from London and the American forces stationed at Marsworth. It did less well later, due to competition from Aylesbury and Hemel Hempstead, and closed in 1958, the last film shown being *Gunfight at the OK Corral*. Efforts were made for further projects, both with cinema and live theatre, but by the end of 1978 the building was demolished and ten flats where built on the site and given the name Regal Court.

Tring Town Football Club. Back row: Arthur 'Junky' Baldwin, Bert Hare, 'Choice' Higby, Jimmy Webb, 'Butler' Howlett. Middle row: Doug Westcroft, Fred Reeves, Stan Hart. Front row: ? Gomm, Tony Musgrave, George Connell, 'Chuckle' Brooks, Bob Cato.

Tring Park Cricket Club 1920 First XI. Back row: H. Challen (scorer), Leonard Hawkins, Reg Honour, Harold Saunders, Arthur Hedges, D. Hart, Mr Prior (umpire). Middle row: 'Teddy' Clarke, Arthur Butcher (captain), C.P. Cole. Front row: Tom Blundell, George Bell, Revd T.V. Garnier, T. Pratt.

Tring Park Cricket Club 1932 Wednesday XI. The Wednesday XI consisted of players who had local shops or businesses that involved having to work on a Saturday. Standing: L. Brooks (scorer), Albert Kempster, Harry Baker, L. King, Horace Bandy, Reg Sallery, A. Fulks, C. Batchelor (umpire). Sitting: S. Lovegrove, Arthur Waldock, Fred Cox (captain), R. Cosier, Jack Kingham.

The Tring Park Cricket Club 1951 Second XI. Back row: R. Darwin (umpire), Stan Scales, F. Wilson, H. Dixon, P. Earner, Bill Green, F. Fisk. Sitting: C. Batchelor, William Kew, Fred Howlett (captain), Doug Westcott, L. Corbett. Front: L. Hitchings (scorer).

The Tring Girl Guides at their camp site at Hang Hill, near Tring, during the Second World War. Some of these girls came to Tring as evacuees at the beginning of the war. Back row: Miss Howson, Lily Jaycock, Hazel Bowman, Barbara Verney, Joan Killick, Betty Warwick, Joyce Rowe, Joan Wright, Pamela Nye, Elaine Berry, Jean Singer?, Barbara Heath, Jill Walters, Thelma Nye, Florence Goddard. Front row: Ruth Norman, Frances Bellamy, Josie Simmons, Peggy Warwick, Janice Gower, Christine List.

Cubs and scouts at the Chiltern Bus Company's Tring Garage in Western Road on Saturday,1 July 1933, waiting to go to the County Rally at Hatfield House. The rally was to welcome the Chief Scout and Lady Baden-Powell. In charge was SM. Nicol Stenhouse and some of the boys were J. Tarmer, L. Symons, J. Deverill, J. Howlett, Rover Squires, ? Duff, ? Lawrence,? Brady, L. Tarmer, ? Plum, Mr Wright of Wright & Wright kindly lent a van free of charge to take the troop's gear.

1st Tring Scout Group in front of the bonfire they built for the Silver Jubilee celebrations in May 1935, on the downs above Tring.

1st Tring Scout Group at Kingsdown summer camp 1955. Back row: Roland Jeffery, Leslie Horne, Ralph Wood, Len Cousins, Phil Gibbs, Trevor Ellis, Robert Collins, Alan Horne, Mervyn Bone, Roger Evans, Malcolm Hewitt, Pat Deverell, Jack Kingham. Front row: Ron Kindel, Terry Childs, Keith Crannage, Dave West, Eddie Golightly, Derek Read, David Gunn, Tony Read.

The British Legion band and members, some in fancy dress, parade down the High Street, in 1935, on their way to the Park for their fete. Mr George Sayer was Bandmaster and Mr A.G Crocker and Mrs E.A. Rance carried the standards. The policeman is standing on the corner where, for many years, you would not have been able to take a photograph without including a member of Tring's police force.

The Tring British Legion band photographed here in full uniform for the first time, after taking part in the special church parade in connection with the Patronal Festival of Tring parish church in 1934. Back, by the flag: ? Bradding, -?-. Back row, standing: ? Goodall, Stan Barber,? Copcutt, -?-, -?-, Albert Clarkson, George Sayer (bandmaster), -?-, Sid Lovegrove, ? Booth,? Cooper, Fred Baldwin, ? Rance, George Bradding. Front row, sitting: Ray Sayer, -?-, ? Palmer, Arthur Bradding, -?-, Sam Marshall, Fred Copcutt, ? Hearn, G. Doody, Jack Hearn. Front row boys: A. Copcutt, -?-.

This photograph was taken around 1929 by the local photographer, Mr George Bell. While out for a walk he met the 'Henry Street Gang' and persuaded them to pose for his camera. They are: (at back) Ernest Foster, Len Smith, Gary Harrop, Arthur Keen, Alfie Hearn, Ken Smith, Phillip Keen, Len Collins, Les Foster.

A group of Tring people at the 'Old Tyme Market' held in the High Street in 1952. Adults: Fanny Mead, Mrs Hollands, Freddie Welch, Nora Grace, Ann ?. Children: Janet ? , Heather Grace, Ann Grace, John Grace, Ann ? . In the background can be seen Bob Metcalfe and Tom Grace.

Tring Young Wives outing in 1955. Back row: Mrs C. Organ, Mrs Lila Jennings , Mrs 'Snowy' Hewett, Mrs Lisa Lockhart, Mrs Organ's mother, Mrs Tite, Mrs Bishop, -?-, Mrs G Hall. Front row: Mrs Eirlys Thomas, Mrs Peggy Slemeck, Mrs Janie Standen, Mrs Grace Hodge, Mrs Connie Wright, Mrs Molly Benson, Mrs Kath Jelly.

There was a Tring Camera Club in the early years of the twentieth century, as existing prize medals of the time show. It was obviously dissolved later and was not revived until the early 1960s, when the members met in the Hall in Tabernacle Yard in Akeman Street. They now meet in the Vestry Hall. This photograph shows a portrait session in the late sixties. Those with cameras are: Leslie Bristow, Len Coulham, Dave Kingham, Neville Pearman, and Hugh Bass. Others in the group are Dick Bignell, Melvin Nash, John Waterton, Margaret Bass, Bob Hummer, and Robert Vickers.

Five

Schooldays

A pre-1920s photograph of Tring schoolboys. The group includes: Bob Potter, Fred Reeve, G. Bradding, W. Gomm, ? Higby, ? Hearn, Reg Potter and S. Hearn. Bob and Reg Potter later had a shop in the High Street selling paints and decorating materials.

Above: An early photograph of Ivy Cottage, Miss Wilson's 'dame school' in Western Road. It was there before the National School and schoolmaster's house that can be seen in the background. The children would have been taught the skills of straw plaiting. The gate on the right is the entrance to Parsonage Farm.

Left: A later view of Ivy Cottage, then occupied by Thomas Pusey. In the doorway we see Mr Pusey, a widower, who lived in the cottage with his granddaughter, Annie. He was the estate carpenter for Pendley and his workshop can be seen on the left.

Opposite above: Prospect House School in the 1890s, viewed from the downs. To the left are houses in Park Road and to the right the Louisa Cottages, when only the first part had been built, and beyond them is the museum. Prospect House was demolished as part of the Rothschild clearance scheme and the site is now an open field for horse grazing.

A closer view of Prospect House School. This was a thriving boys school maintaining a high standard of education. Dr Clarabut, the New Mill pastor, was headmaster, followed by Mr Mark Young. In the 1891 census the school had eleven boarders, most coming from London and the home counties. When the buildings were demolished the school was moved to Brookfield, when the headmaster was Mr Maull.

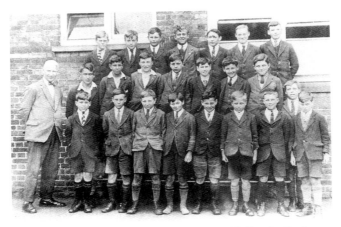

A class of Tring School in the 1920s. The master is Mr Douglas Harrison. He came to the school in 1925 and was appointed headmaster of Tring Church of England mixed school in 1931. He died in 1942 shortly after his retirement. Back row: Cyril Batchelor, Charlie Kempster, William Budd, George Prentice, William Barber, Harold Bowley, Henry Porter Christopher. Middle row: Lionel Tyrrel, Roland Austin: Jack Harding, Charles Mildred, Les Picton, Wally Crockett, Harold Randall. Front row: Maurice Mansfield, Joseph Edwin, Jack Ide, B. Miller, C. Paget, Charlie Kempster. William Edwin, ? Nutkins, George Ginger.

Tring schoolboys c. 1926-7. Back row: Dicky Brandon, Peter Rush, Sidney Bullock, Joe Brooks, Ian Marks, Bob Fincher, Frank Gower, G. Smith, Dave Davis, Donald Theed, Basil Everett, Peter Bell. Middle row: A. Watkins, C. Knapp, Albert Higby, A. Caldwell, F. Witson, Charles Blundell, Les Tarmer, Tony Griffin, Harold Wilkins, Graham Clarkson, Peter Bowley. Front row: A. Cross, Ron Emery, Charles Meek, Reg West, Willy Messenger, Jack Ives, Logan Tapping, Cyril Ginger, Steb Allibone, Chris Batchelor, Sidney Eldridge.

she taught me.

Tring junior mixed scholarship winners of 1936. Back row: Miss Smith, Miss Baker, Miss Lacey. Middle row: Arthur Haddon, John Vranch, ? Perkins, John Chapman, Peter Harrowell. Front row: Audrey Mansfield, Barbara Kettle, Vera Gurney, Terry Buckingham.

Tring School group of 1950. Back row: Mr Hamilton, ? Smith, Vicky Collins, Enid Hill, -?-, -?-, Pam Chandler, -?-, Ann Kempster, Neville Kempster, Brian Dover, Miss Baker. Middle row:-?-, Annie Gascoine, David Kempster, Michael Colby, Paddy Foster, June Welling, Michael Bond, ? Rance, Bruce Messenger, Mavis Fleckney. Front Row: Brenda Mills, John Ashpool, Robin ?, Audrey Bingham, Ann Wright, Leslie Chamberlain, Brenda Lee, -?-, Sadie Wright.

Class of Tring School in the early 1950s with teacher Mr Les Tarmer. Back row: Phyllis Hart, Pamela Burney, Jean Sayer, Ken Verney, Stephen Hearn, Pamela Sheen, Eunice Wander, June Flitney. Third row: Joe Kempster, Dennis Gunn, Alan Rance, Derek Freeman, Alfie Welling, Brian Mortlock, Dennis Burch. Second row: Evelyn Keen, Marion Burch, Gwen Weedon, Maureen Green, Mavis Rance, Mary Bethell, Avis Butler. Front row: Clive Halsey, Ray Smith, John Drake, Harry Jeffs, Kenny Rance, Peter Flitney, Michael Cox.

Tring School group of 1954 with teachers Miss Baker and Miss Buckoke. Back row: Desmond Anning, Heather Halsey, Frances Lowdell, Tony Baker, Marion Ginger, Sandra Hearn, Barry Webster, Barry Wells, Andy McCallister, Jimmy Carter, Third row: -?-, Jill Organ, Janine Mitchell, -?-, -?-, ? Higby, -?-, -?-, -?-, -?-, Brian Gregory, -?- , Second row: Alan Smith, Angela Bateman, Raymond Huey, -?-, Jean Nash, -?-, Brenda Smith, Paul Wright, Michael Standen, -?-. Front row: Pamela Philpott, -?-, Terry Ives, ? Major, -?-, -?-, Christine Cousens.

Tring Junior School in 1956 with their teacher Mrs Hamilton. Back row: Adam Wainwright, Graham Broad, Derek Hearn, Andrew ?, Alan Lawrence, Bill Dwight, Steven Gregory, Frankie Phillips, Gareth Noble. Third row: Susan Elliot, Jacqueline Barnes, Ann Garrett, Mary Hinton, Elizabeth Miller, Lynn Wright, Terry Oliver, Simon Warren, Second row: Penny Standen, Hilary Prouse, Doreen Pearsall, Valerie ?, Beryl ?, Linda Hoare, Sally Jones, Annette Seabrook, Christine Chapman. Front row: John Nutkins, Graham ?, Geoffrey Gort, Nicholas Harris, Benjamin ?, Alistair Keay, -?-, Nigel Rodwell, Anthony Hartley.

Tring School group with teachers Mr and Mrs Stanley Thomas. Back row: Derek Stratton, Raymond Hooper, Roland Ginger, Alan Horne, Stephen Humphreys, Robin Desborough, Barry Wooton, Richard Stratford. Middle row: Susan Pitcher, Brian Johnson, Keith Messenger, David Prentice, Les Casemore, John Cutler, Ian Johnson, Robert Denby. Front row: -?-, Shirley Bailey, Dean Horne, Sheila Simmonds, Kay Jelley, Jill Campbell, Pat Newton, Brenda Deeley, Pamela Worrall.

Junior school children in the 1970s playing outside the schoolmaster's house when the school was still in the High Street. This house and the school were later demolished and replaced by the library and car park.

At Tring School, the popular headmaster, Mr Stanley Thomas, is being given a noisy send-off by his pupils on his retirement in 1968. With him is his wife, Eirlys, who still lives in Tring and is remembered affectionately by many ex-pupils, as she was also one of the school's teachers.

An aerial view of the old High Street School and the masters house, showing the new Bishop Wood School in the background. The old buildings were later demolished to make way for the new library.

When the new school was built to replace the old High Street building, a small swimming pool was included, here being enjoyed by some young pupils. When the larger indoor pool was built at the senior school at Mortimer Hill (available to the public out of school hours), the use of this one was discontinued.

Popular school teacher Bob Hummer, with a group of his pupils at Bishop Wood School. As well as his school interests, Bob devoted a lot of his spare time to the Tring Scouts and was Scoutmaster for many years. He was also a very keen photographer, taking several of the photographs in this book, and was Chairman of Tring Camera Club from its early days, a position he held for the rest of his life. Some of the children pictured here are Paul Gilson, Stephen Adams, Ian Scott and Tim Dureall.

Early days of the Secondary Modern School at Mortimer Hill. A lot of the buildings in this 1955 photograph are temporary huts which were later replaced by the brick ones that stand today. Here the flourishing school garden can be seen before it made way for more buildings and tennis courts. Now the school is almost surrounded by housing estates.

Six

Churches
and Places of Worship

Tring Parish Church in the 1960s. Parts of the church date back to the fifteenth century, though most has been added to over the years and major restorations were done in the nineteenth century. A striking monument in the north aisle is that of Sir William and Lady Gore of Tring Park. Sir William is dressed in the robes of the Lord Mayor of London.

Left: The interior of Tring church. The pews in the nave were made in the 1860s by James Forsyth of London, who also made the pulpit which was given by former patrons, the students of Christ Church College, Oxford. Most of the stained glass windows are by the famous Victorian firm of C.E. Kempe.

Below: The Old vicarage was built in Victorian times but in a mock Jacobean style. In 1891, the Vicar in residence was the Revd William Quennell, a widower, who lived with his sister and daughter. It was purchased by the Sutton Housing Trust and remains virtually unaltered. Buildings were added to make the Trust's offices and the Anglican-Methodist hall. The complex won the Royal Institute of British Architects award in 1976.

Opposite above: The Baptist Chapel. One of the earliest in Hertfordshire, the first chapel was built at Frogmore End, now Frogmore Street, in 1751. It was described as 'one of the queerest, stuffiest, ugliest little chapels you can conceive of'. It has a grave yard in front which the road turns to avoid'. In the late 1830s the building was enlarged to front the road and here in the 1970s is being used as an antique shop. It is now a private house.

A new Baptist church was built late in the nineteenth century in the High Street. Many ministers served their communities for a considerable number of years including the Revd William Sexton (1838-1874) and the Revd Charles Pearce (1874-1920). The United Free Baptist Church, completed in 1886 comprised a church and lecture hall, and a new organ was bought in 1949 to replace one that had been there since the beginning of the century.

The Quaker Meeting House at the end of Akeman Street, in Park Street. There were Quakers in Tring in the seventeenth century but they suffered considerable persecution. By the cottage was a burial ground where some eighty Quakers were buried. The cottage was demolished in the nineteenth century and all that remains now is the ground with a monument inscribed: 'This enclosure was used by the Society of Friends as a burying ground from 1678-1809'. 'In our church is neither epitaph nor monument, tombstone nor names, only the turf we tread and a few natural graves' (Wordsworth).

The Tring Salvation Army band c. 1930. Back row: Stan Barber, Albert Hart, Arthur Brown (flagman), George Baker, George Smith (RAF Halton). Third row: Frank Gascoine, Ray Sayer, Will Gascoine, Harold Sayer, George Sayer (bandmaster), J. Finney, Mr McCurdy, George Impey. Second row: Miss Daisy Gascoine, -?-, -?-, -?-. Front row: Jim Impey, Arthur Sayer. A Salvation Army band still plays in the town and they meet in their citadel in Albert Street.

Akeman Street Baptist Chapel from a drawing of 1808 when the meeting house was built. Pastor Glover made the chapel very popular and it became known as 'Glovers Chapel', attracting members from the New Mill Chapel. The building has been enlarged and improved but looks much the same and is still in regular use as a place of worship.

St Marthas church was built around 1880, probably by Carpenter and Ingelow who were at the time working on the parish church. In the early 1900s the west arm was built with dark weatherboarding, and much later a brick porch was added. It was later registered for Methodist marriages, the first wedding being that of Miss Susan Wilshire on 26 January 1974. The big tree was a victim of the gales in January 1990.

The Primitive Methodist chapel in Langdon Street was built in the latter half of the nineteenth century, the stone-laying ceremony taking place on 22 September 1870. Although the membership was not very large and the chapel suffered bomb damage in the Second World War, the church reached its centenary in 1970 and there were two weeks of celebrations. Sadly, soon after that, it was decided that the membership could not continue to finance the repairs that were necessary, and when the Langdon Street Methodists were invited, in 1975, to share St Marthas in Park Road with the Anglicans, they were pleased to do so. After the demolition of the chapel a pair of semi-detached houses were built to fill the space.

New Mill Baptist Church. There are records to suggest that Baptists worshipped in New Mill in the seventeenth century but the first chapel was built in 1775, when Henry Blaine was the minister. In 1818, when Daniel Clarabut was pastor, the present church was built and a school room, which can be seen behind it, was built in 1897. The photograph was taken very early in the twentieth century.

Seven

Services

This horse-drawn fire engine was in use for almost 200 years, not being replaced by a motorised model until the 1930s. The horses belonged to Mr Gower, the coal merchant, who is here seen driving them.

Here the Tring Fire Brigade, and members of the council, pose by their new Model T Ford fire engine. Back row: -?-, Duke Welling. Middle row: Mr Reeves, Edward Brittain, Fred Rance, Bill Cooper, -?-, George Putnam, Bill Keele, -?-. Front row: Mr W.N. Mead, -?-, John Bagnall, John Bly, -?-, Hubert Gurney (seated) Clerk of the Council, Mr Baldock (ex PC), George Goddard.

Tring Fire Brigade with their new Leyland fire engine photographed at the Silk Mill in Brook Street. Top row: Eddie Brackley, -?-, Bertie Wright. Middle row: George Hinton, Sid Lovell, William Keele, George Goodliffe. Front row: Mr Sear, S. Harrop, William Welling, George Putnam, Fred Rance, W. Richardson, Harry Bull.

A line up of Tring firemen being presented with long service medals by the Chairman of the Council, Capt. Donald Brown. Front row: William Keele, Eddie Brackley, Harry Bull, George Hinton, Sid Lovell, William Welling. In the back row are: George Goodliffe (concealed behind Mr Keele), S. Harrop, Fred Rance. At the front: Captain George Putnam.

Tring Fire Brigade outside the purpose-built station in Brook Street, and behind is the new Bedford fire engine. When the station was in the Market House, on the corner of Akeman Street, the entrance was so narrow that this fire engine was fitted with rubber bumpers to protect it from scratches. Left to right: Jock Graffen, Ken Carlisle, Bill Giddings, Doug Sinclair, Paddy Foster, Charlie Cummings, Tom Saunders, Roy Robinson, Wally Rance, Dennis Bradding, Dudley Fulks, John Foskett, Bill Gosling.

Tring and District 'Special' Police in 1940s. Back row: -?-, George Evans, -?-, -?-, William Jeffery, Mr Hamilton, Eric Mead, Arthur Edwards. Middle row: -?-, Frank Rogers, -?-, -?-, -?-, Percy Bagnall, -?-, Stanley Thomas, R. George Wright. Front row. Starmer Collins, -?-, Harold Grace, Charles Bushell, -?-, -?-, Tom Pratt, Jack Wright, -?-, Mr Green.

Tring Red Cross 1946. Back row: Mrs Badrick, Molly Newman, -?-, Agnes Gurney, Gertrude Jones, Hilda Tyler, Gladys Hull, Nora Grace, -?-, Betty Dell, Gladys Cato, Mrs McDermott. Middle row: -?-, Mrs Mead, Miss Bowlby, -?-, Elsie Batchelor, Mrs Chapman, Mrs Simmonds, Kathy Akers, Joyce Warwick, Lily Jaycock, Gladys Price, Mrs Carrington, Mrs Cartwright (Wilstone). Front row: Mrs Rolfe, Mrs Flower, Joan Cole, Dr. Knox, Phyllis Wright, Mary Bowlby, Dolly Keen, Mrs Marshall, Mrs Scaby.

Tring St Johns Ambulance Brigade in the 1940s. Back row: Tom Hedges, George Bell, John Copcutt, Bill Capel, Peter Capel, Wally Rance, Stan Harrop, Mr Budd, Mr Bagnall. Front row: Doug Saunders, Tom Moy, Jock Blyth, -?-, Frank Rance.

Young members of the St Johns Ambulance Brigade c. 1960. Back row: Rosemary Prentice, Geraldine Gordon, Margaret Kempson, Janet Lovell, Susan Sayer, Jacqueline Kempster, Rosemary Stone, Evelyn Tippett, Janet Reeves, -?-. Front row: Penelope Southgate, -?-, Mrs Whittaker, Rosemary Hamilton, Delia ?.

The Tring Council water carrier, with Billy Mills, filling up at the water hydrant in Charles Street. The shop in the background is a drapers, ran for many years by Miss Ives. It is now a private house.

Having filled up the tank the carrier can be seen laying the dust in Tring High Street. On a hot day the children would follow the cart to enjoy a cool shower. On the right of the photograph can be seen part of the Rose and Crown Hotel.

Eight

Tring Park
and the Rothschilds

The Park Gates. Tring.

The gates to Tring Park decorated to welcome Nathaniel Rothschild's younger son, Charles, and his bride, Hungarian-born Rozsika von Wertheimstein, after their marriage in 1907. Rozsika was an athletic young lady, she was the Hungarian lawn tennis champion and an accomplished ice skater, but she settled down well in England and she and Charles had four children. The eldest daughter, Miriam, is well known as a biologist, interested in flora and fauna, as her Uncle Walter had been, and also for her writings about the Rothschild families.

The Tring Park gates from the inside, showing the High Street in the background. These beautiful gates, made by Gilbert Grace, sadly went for scrap during the Second World War. Notice on the left hand side the Old Market House still stands in front of the church. The shop with the blinds down is Ellimans, drapers and agents for the County Fire Insurance Co.

The Park Street entrance to the mansion. The iron gates have now gone, another casualty of the war effort, but the gate house and the other houses still remain. Alongside the gate house runs the public footpath to the park, now under management of the Woodland Trust, having been purchased by Dacorum Borough Council in 1994, 'to preserve it for the people of Tring, as a historic parkland and an important part of the Chiltern countryside'.

The mansion as it was before its purchase by the Rothschilds. It was built for Henry Guy, groom of the bedchamber to King Charles II and is attributed to Sir Christopher Wren. The Tring Park Estate was sold to Baron Lionel de Rothschild for £230,000 in 1872.

Tring mansion after Baron Rothschild had it altered more to his taste, a sort of 'cladding' over the original building, and another wing was added. It was not to everyone's liking and was described by some as looking like a large hospital and a well-windowed Victorian prison. It is now home of the Arts Educational School and is virtually unaltered.

Left and below: The two members of the Rothschild family who had the greatest influence on Tring. Seen here on his hunter is Nathaniel Mayer (1840-1915) who built a lot of the town as it still is today, and his son Lionel Walter (1868-1937), here in his sixties, who founded the world famous museum.

Tring Museum after it was opened to the public in 1892. The cottage in front is that of Mr Alfred Minall, Walter Rothschild's taxidermist, and his family. It was built by Walter's father as part of his coming-of-age present. Walter, when only twelve years of age, dreamed of having his own museum and in 1880 made Alfred Minall his curator, with his workshop in Albert Street.

The Bothy on the London Road when it was used by Lord Rothschild's gardeners. The word 'bothy', dating back to the eighteenth century, is said to mean 'a small hut or cottage, especially for housing labourers'. This does not adequately describe this building which was well built and survives to this day, although its future may be at risk if plans for a supermarket on the site go ahead.

Tring Show in Tring Park. The history of Tring Show dates back to 1841 but it started in a very small way at Tring station, later moving to the Park. It was originally held in October but was changed to August in the first Lord Rothschild's time and by then was attracting around 20,000 visitors.

Lord Rothschild was particularly interested in the breeding of heavy horses and had a stud farm outside Tring, where Thomas Fowler was in charge. Here several elegant ladies are watching the heavy horse class at Tring Show, but the show programme stated that the mansion gardens would be open for the enjoyment of those ladies not interested in agricultural matters. There was also a barber available for the gentleman.

Above and below: Tring Show became the largest one day show in the country and there were classes for all types of farm animals as well as dog trials and show jumping. The show was not held in Tring Park after 1939.

Lord Rothschild's stud farm at West Leith in the countryside outside Tring. These buildings have now been converted into comfortable private houses.

Town Farm, where Mr Dawe lived, provided the site where Lord Rothschild built Home Farm for his agent Mr Richardson Carr.

Home Farm photographed in the 1950s when it housed the Moss family. It was the home of Lord Walter Rothschild for the last few years, before his death in 1937. During the Second World War it was used as a maternity home run by volunteers. After the war it was sold to Flight-Lieutenant Kirby, who made various additions, including an ornamental pool with a fountain and two life-size female figures, all built in the centre of the farm yard.

Mr Richardson Carr, photographed at a sale in the farmyard; he was the agent for the estate and the occupant of Home Farm. The 1891 census lists him, aged thirty four, with his wife, Mary, daughter Catherine, then aged eight, and three servants. The roadway to the house is still known to older people as 'Carr's Drive'.

Left and below: Tring has had several well known citizens, but perhaps none more famous than Stirling and Pat Moss who lived at Home Farm, then renamed White Cloud Farm. Stirling, the top racing driver of his day, was the first Briton to win the Mille Miglia, in May 1955, and won his first Grand Prix two months later. In July 1957 he won the British Grand Prix at Aintree, the first Britain to do so since 1923, and in the same year won the Italian Grand Prix at Monza. Pat, equally well known in the showjumping world, was the 'Leading Juvenile Jumper of the Year' at Harringay in 1950 on her pony 'Brandy of White Cloud'. She progressed to senior jumping and was with the British Team for fifteen years, two of her best horses being 'Geronimo' and 'Danny Boy'. She combined riding with rally-driving and was European Champion for six years; later giving up show jumping to concentrate on driving.

Nine

Tring in the Wars

Father Christmas distributing gifts to the evacuees in Albert Street in 1939. The little boy in the spotted hat is Charlie 'Tarpy' Rance; the identities of the twin girls and Father Christmas are not known. The boy and girl behind Santa are brother and sister Doug and Mavis Sinclair, the boy with fair hair in front of Mavis is brother Peter Sinclair. The boy in the dark cap is ? Brandon, and the boy in front with the light cap is David Mills. The boy on the far right is Ivor Mills.

Although Private 'Jacko' Osborne served with the 58th Northamptonshire Regiment and was the first soldier in the regiment to win the Victoria Cross, his funeral took place in Wigginton as he had lived there for so many years. He won his VC at Wesselroom in 1881 during the Boer War. He died in 1928 aged seventy-one. The photograph shows the coffin being loaded on a gun carriage by six pall bearers from the 2nd Northamptonshire Regiment with almost everyone in the village turning out to see the event. The Revd T. Drake conducted the service in the church.

Dedication of the memorial to Private James Osborne VC. The group include Mr and Mrs Poulton, Private Osborne's daughter and son-in-law with their baby. During the Boer War Private Osborne was sent out with a friend, Private Mayes, and another soldier to cut some forage for the horses when the Boers attacked them. Private Mayes horse was killed and he was shot in the leg. The other man was shot dead. Private Osborne galloped back to the camp but finding that Private Mayes had not followed he galloped back, picked up his wounded comrade and, miraculously avoiding bullets, got them both safely back. Both soldiers survived the rest of the war and although Private Mayes died before Private Osborne, his two children, Mr George Mayes and Mrs J.H. Brookes, attended the funeral at Wigginton.

Private Edward Barber VC was in the 1st Battalion Grenadier Guards and was the son of William and Sarah Ann Barber and was the only Tring-born soldier to receive the Victoria Cross. The award was for his conspicuous bravery at Neave Chappell on 12 March 1915. The citation reads: 'He ran speedily in front of the Grenade Company, to which he belonged and threw bombs at the enemy with such effect that a very large number of German soldiers at once surrendered. When the grenade party reached Private Barber they found him quite alone and unsupported with the enemy surrendering all around him'. He did not know of his award, however, as he was killed in action the same day, said to have been 'picked off by a German sniper'.

Digging for the Second World War air raid shelters in Tring High Street. In the background the timbered building is No.8 High Street – 'Oasis'. The white building, one of the oldest in Tring, is now a restaurant. Where these shelters stood is now the car park and site of the Friday market.

Filling sandbags outside the Market House in Akeman Street. On the left is Mr Bull, the foreman, next to him is George Turner. The man holding the sack is 'Happy' Adams. The young man above him is Harry 'Splash' Kempster and the other young man on the bags, with the waistcoat, is Joe Kempster. The man bending over is 'Knock' Eggleton and the boy on the bags to the right is Harry Mills.

Tring ARP rescue section photographed outside the stable block at Tring Park. Back row:
Maurice Bradding, Bill Jones, Bert Archer, Don Cartwright, -?-, Nat Gower, Bill Budd,
Fred Cox, Mr Nutkins. Middle row: Bill Lovell, Fred Copcutt, Ted Bagnall, Fred Jakeman,
Harry Bull, Jimmy Attryde, Fred Nutkins, -?-, Benjamin Gower. Front row: Bert Potter, George
Copcutt, Arthur 'Junky' Baldwin, Joe Kempster, Tom Grace, Arnold Halsey, Charles Ginger,
Wally Rance, Tom Moy, G. Bradding.

Tring ARP. Back row: -?-, Bob Hedges, -?-, -?-, -?-, -?-, Fred Hurdle, Sid Horne, Mr Desborough, -?-,
-?-, -?-. Third row: John Bingham, Edgar Bagnall, -?-, Mr Gibbs, Jim Finney, Cyril Howlett, Ernest
Clark, -?-, -?-, -?-, -?-, Mr Higgs, Albert Spencer, Ernest Childs, -?-, -?-. Second row: -?-, -?-, -?-, -?-, -?-,
Hubert G. Gurney, -?-, Mr Vranch, -?-, Harry Bull, Jack Hummerston, -?-, -?-, Miss Pearsall, Delia
Henderson. Front row: Les Parslow, -?-, Mr Kenyon-Bell, Sid Luck, Edward Bell, Sid Rance, -?-,
-?-, -?-, Frank Rance, George Rance, -?-, Mr Bradding.

A parade of civilian volunteers in Western Road in 1939. In the uniformed group on the front are Reg Sallery, 'Choice' Higby, Tom Fulks and Leon Baker. Either side of Reg are Fred Fleckney and Will Higby. The group on the left side include Mary Kemp, with son Roy, in the pram; Alice Church with son Bob; Mr Harry Kempster and Mrs Kempster with son Joe.

Part of the 1939 parade of volunteers along the Western Road. These are the Air Raid Wardens with Mr Vranch (of Cash & Co.) in front, the man on the left of that front group is Freddy Hurdle (manager of the post office).

Men of the Auxiliary Fire Service lead civilian volunteers in the parade along Western Road.

More volunteers in Western Road.

Local children also became involved with the war effort, here we see Tring school boys digging ARP trenches for the school in the meadow next to the playground.

The children of New Mill can be seen selling their sacks of herbs to the collector. Herb gathering was essential during the war as herbs for medicines could not be imported as they had been. The children were only paid a few pence per pound but, with the exception of nettles, picking herbs was not an unpleasant job and the children could feel they were helping the war effort. This photograph, taken in July 1944, shows Meads flour mills in the background.

Tring Home Guard, 7C (18) Company, Platoon (No. 3). Photographed in front of Tring Mansion. Back row: Frank Kent, Fred Edwards, -?-, -?-, Derek Putty, -?-. Forth row: -?-, -?-, -?-, Len 'Sassa' Wright, Reg Potter, -?-, Bob Kempster, -?-, -?-. Third row: Mr Cook, ? Bell, Len Wren, -?-, Les Goodson, Tommy Blackburn, -?-, Ivan Wright, 'Tich' Routley. Second row: -?-,-?-, B. Kemp, Don Roberts, -?-, Bert Allen, -?-, -?-, -?-, -?-. First row: -?-, Joe Budd, Albert Clarkson, Sgt. Bowers, -?-, -?-, -?-, -?-, -?-, -?-, -?-. Front: Fred Gray, Stan Hall, Percy Hart, 'Bek' Jakeman, -?-, -?-, G. Rance.

HMS *Aeolus*. (Aeolus: Greek God of the Winds). This picture of the staff of HMS *Aeolus* was taken in the grounds of Tring Mansion. The depot was at 51-52 High Street, Tring, where Metcalfe's hardware shop is today. They supplied kites and balloons to dockyards in the UK and abroad. These were transferred to ships, mainly merchant shipping, who flew them to combat low flying attacking aircraft. The balloons were like small barrage balloons and the kites were made of canvas with bamboo struts. Back row: Eric Cox, Phil Watts, -?-, -?-, Len Bull, -?-, -?-, Doug Hughes, -?-, Mr Brackett, -?-, -?-, -?-, Jim Fowler. Middle row: -?-, Mr Rance, Charlie Finch, Nancy Nutkins, Phyllis Gates, -?-, Arthur Church, George Reynolds, -?-, -?-, -?-, -?-, -?-, Joy Rance, Les Doughty, Phyllis Nutkins. Front row, sitting: -?-, -?-, -?-, -?-, Miss Scott (secretary), -?-, Lt. Commander Hamer (paymaster), Cmdr Boorman, Lt. Danson, -?-, Mr Russell (civilian manager), Vera Gurney, -?-, Audrey Mansfield, -?-.

Above: Volunteer, retained and AFS at the end of the war in 1945. Back row: J. Dwight, Mr Wright, -?-, E. Rolfe, Frank Smith, E. Higby, Harry Saunders, Leon Baker, Eddie Brackley, C. Gregory. Third row: Mr Robinson, F. Whittle, Ron Hicks, S. Stevens, Mr Dumpleton, J. Wood, Arthur Higby, Mr Burch, -?-, Arthur Flitney, Archie Fulks, A. West. Second row: Fred Chandler, R. Cousins, William Barber, H. Cutler, Mr Gregory, Dick Green, Bert Nutkins, Mr Sear, Tom Fulks, Ray Pheasant, Mr Kennedy, Mr Wander, George Hinton, M. Foster. Front row: Jock Wilson, Mary Luck, Miss Warburton, Kathy Gower, Jack Lines, Reg Sallery, Mr Burton, George Goodliffe, Harry Bull, H. Harrop, E. Haddon, ? Hart.

Left: The National Savings chart on the wall of Wheeler Brothers' shop in the High Street. Wheeler Bros. was the chief selling centre for National Saving Certificates during 'Salute the Soldier Week'. During this week alone, having previously raised nearly £750,000, Tring raised a further £121,564. This represented £24 per head of the population, a large sum in 1944. Painting in the Spitfire is Harry Fennimore from Bushell Bros.

Ten

Public Houses and Inns

The Green Man, No.5 Lower High Street. John Philby brewed here in 1846 but by 1851 the inn keeper was Jane Philbey, a widow. Also at the inn was Jane's nephew, twelve-year-old John Meager, who was the publican in 1870. John Woodman kept the inn from 1878 to 1895. He was a widower and was assisted by his daughters, Mary and Kate. The inn was used by many local societies for their annual dinners; the Tring Association dinner in 1887 cost £4 for twenty people. The Green Man was pulled down by Lord Rothschild in 1895.

The old Rose and Crown, at the beginning of the twentieth century. It was an old coaching inn and stood level with the other buildings until it was demolished by the Rothschilds around 1905. In the 1851 census Sarah Northwood was the inn keeper with six living-in staff. In the 1890s the hotel keeper was Jabez Thorn assisted by his wife, Caroline, their son Jesse, and their daughter-in-law Annie. The building on the left of the photograph is the gatehouse of Tring Mansion and contained a mechanism for opening and closing the large ornamental gates.

The hotel photographed after it had been rebuilt by the Rothschild Estate 1905-06. It was built to William Huckvale's design and on its completion was made over to the Hertfordshire Public House Trust, forerunner of Trust House Forte. It continued to be used by visitors to the mansion, including Prince Edward, the Prince of Wales, in 1935. The shop on the right hand side was for many years De Fraines, stationers, newsagents and booksellers, and was the branch office of the *Bucks Herald*.

The Robin Hood in Brook Street early in the twentieth century, next door to William Bly's furniture shop. It was a seventeenth-century building but much altered and restored. In 1806 the landlord was William Tapping and in the 1850s it was Ann Tompkins; by 1870 Henry Becket was in charge. The 1891 census lists the licensed victualler as Charles Harrison, assisted by his wife Sarah. They obtained their supplies from Roberts & Wilson of Ivinghoe.

This is one of the oldest surviving public houses in Tring. In 1611 Henry Geary was before the Justices for keeping the Bell without a licence and a few years later for drunkenness. In the 1660s tokens were issued by Hastings Parrot of the Bell, as small change was in short supply. Some of these rare coins still exist, also those of other tradesmen in the town. In the 1870s and 80s Joseph Norris was the publican; later in the century John Evans, followed by David Hart, and in the first two decades of the twentieth century Edgar Short was in residence.

The original George Hotel in Frogmore Street was described as a small hostelry and corn chandlers held in 1806 by Joseph Tompkins and by William Clark in 1830. It was rebuilt and enlarged to reach the High Street at the end of the nineteenth century by the Aylesbury Brewery Company. The building was more recently used by John Hervery, a mail order clothing business, and is now an estate agent.

The Britannia, Western Road, was built by John Brown of Tring Brewery in the 1840s, chiefly to cater for the navvies working on the London to Birmingham Railway. In 1870 the publican was Charles Smith and in the 1890s Job Archer was there with his wife, Rebecca. The Britannia is now a private home renamed Norfolk House.

Right: The Anchor, Western Road in the early 1970s. It is still a pub and looks much the some today. Built in the nineteenth century it was then a beerhouse and in 1891 was kept by Alfred Barber and his wife, Jane; at the beginning of the twentieth century William Wells was in charge. Kellys directory of 1933 lists Samuel Nightingale Jnr. beer retailer at 25 Western Road.

Below: The Castle in Park Road was built in the nineneenth century and still enjoys a clear view of the downs. The photograph was taken in the late 1960s and the public house has altered little over the years. In 1870 the publican was William Loyd and he was there with his wife, Harriet, until the 1890s. In 1899 the landlord was George Robert Ives and in 1933-37 it was Ephraim Hearn.

The Swan, Akeman Street in the 1930s. It was a popular pub in Victorian times and was frequented by many of the mansion staff and known locally as the 'butlers' pub. In the 1880s Joseph Gurney lived there with his wife, Mary Ann. Some later publicans have been George Murrey, Thomas Scott, Charles Humphreys, Hy Ives, and Tom Saunders. The Swan is now a private house.

Wingrave Road, New Mill. On the right is the Queens Arms public house. In 1891 the publican was thirty-year-old Frederick Philby, who lived there with his wife, Annie, and their one-year-old son, also named Frederick. The Queens Arms, known to locals as 'Red House' closed on 24 February 1974. The council bought the land, demolished the pub and built new houses, calling the road Elizabeth Drive to commemorate the Queen's Silver Jubilee.

Eleven

Nearby Places

An early photograph of Aldbury, one of Hertfordshire's most picturesque villages, which nestles at the foot of rising beechwoods that form part of Ashridge Park, now owned by the National Trust. The magnificent elm tree by the pond, featured for so many years in postcards and photographs, has sadly now gone, the victim of Dutch elm disease.

A view of Aldbury in around 1910, taken from the church tower. The pond can just be seen on the left, and the Memorial Hall on the right. The church of St John the Baptist is partly thirteenth-century, or earlier, and has a flint-faced tower. The village still has a lot of its sixteenth- and seventeenth-century, timber-framed, brick and tile cottages and, although more modern houses have been added, it still retains its old-world charm.

The word 'Aldbury' means old fort in Anglo Saxon and the village was already settled in pre-Saxon times. This photograph, probably taken in the 1930s, shows The Greyhound in the centre. In the 1891 census we see the publican was Rachel Long, a sixty-one-year-old widow. The house to the left was the old post office, and in the nineteenth century it was run by John Dolt and his niece Eliza M. Glenister. On the right one can just see Town Farm where the farm buildings have now been converted into dwellings and the house does mouth watering cream teas.

Pitstone Cross-roads.

Pitstone. It is said that Pitstone was first settled in the Iron Age, and a mammoth tooth, recovered locally, is in the Pitstone Museum. As with other villages, the nearby Icknield Way to East Anglia encouraged settlement. It was once dominated by the Pitstone Cement Works which has now closed. Although part of the area has become a nature reserve, conservationists are now trying to prevent the rest from becoming a huge waste dump. When Samuel Hawkins came to Pitstone in 1808 he started a line of Hawkins farmers at Pitstone Green Farm that has extended to the present day. The farm, today run by Mr Jeff Hawkins, houses the Pitstone Museum.

Church End, Pitstone, early in the twentieth century. These 'two up, two down' cottages housed mainly labourers and their families. The 1891 census records Reuben Wilkins living in one of these small dwellings with his wife and seven children.

The first reference to the Manor of Marsworth was made in the year 970, when Elgive, sister-in-law to Edgar, King of Wessex, wrote that she would leave him in her will the Manor of Marsworth, as well as Wing, Linslade and Haversham. In the Domesday book Marsworth or Missworde as it was written then, was held by Ralph Bassett. In 1739 one third part was sold to William Gore of Tring Park. The remaining portions were later sold to the Bridgewater family and were the property of the Earl Brownlow. The records of All Saints church go back to the sixteenth century although extensive repairs were carried out in the 1800s.

The White Lion, Marsworth. A popular pub on the Grand Union Canal. The 1891 census records that Elizabeth Jellis, a forty-two-year-old widow, was there with her nineteen-year-old son William.

Long Marston in 1903. The shop and cottage beyond are now a pair of private houses. The cottages in the distance are much the same today, but the space between now has a house and the village hall built in it.

Long Marston showing the Station Road-Cheddington Road corner. The gentleman sitting by the front gate is Mr John Chappin. Down the Cheddington Road can be seen the Long Marston Baptist Chapel which was erected in 1869. This view has altered little since this photograph was taken.

Wilstone early in the twentieth century. On the right is the Buckingham Arms, run in 1891 by William Cartwright, living there with his wife and their five children. This is now two private dwellings, though the names still include the word 'Buckingham'. Almost hidden between cottages further down is Wilstone's surviving public house, 'The Half Moon'. The publican in 1891 was James Reeve with his wife Elizabeth and their large family of five daughters and three sons. From 1906 Walter Cartwright was the landlord and, when he was killed in France in 1918, his wife Lavinia was the landlady until her retirement in 1936.

Wilstone showing Long Row on the left hand side with Mrs Denchfield's shop on the corner which is now a private house. The old cottages on the right hand side have since been demolished.

Gubblecote, called Bublecote in the Domesday book, was described as part of the land the Count of Mortain had taken from Tring. This old cottage, at Gubblecote Cross, stands near the place where local records say that Tring chimney-sweep, Thomas Colley, was hanged for the murder of an old lady, Ruth Osbourne, on 24 August 1745. She and her husband were accused of witchcraft and a mob tried to drown them in Long Marston pond. Only Mrs Osbourne died and Colley was accused as a ringleader. The persecution of witches had officially ceased in 1736.

Drayton Beauchamp. Early in the thirteenth century William de Beauchamp held the Manor of Drayton, and although the family only stayed for two generations they gave their name to the village of Drayton Beauchamp. A church was first mentioned in the eleventh century, but the present church dates from the fifteenth century, although the Norman font dates from the twelfth. Baptisms were first registered in 1538, burials in 1567 and marriages in 1541.

The Village, Buckland, near Aston

Above: There was a settlement on the site of Buckland Village centuries before the Normans came, as it had an important position near the Lower Icknield Way, a road dating back to pre-Roman times. It is mentioned in the Domesday Book and has had a series of Lords of the Manor. The church was built in the thirteenth century. It fell into disrepair and might have been lost had it not been taken over by the wealthy, if rather eccentric, Revd Edward Bonus in the nineteenth century. Buckland Common, once part of the parish of Buckland, was, in the 1930s, joined with Cholesbury and Hawridge.

Left: Puttenham, although now a tiny hamlet, was once much larger, the church being the centre of the village with a rector and manor house. The name is derived from the de Puttenhams, the family who occupied the manor for five generations before Queen Elizabeth I came to the throne. The church was first mentioned in the twelfth century, and the fifteenth century tower is one of only two in Hertfordshire with chequer-work formed by limestone and flints. Many local people still remember services and weddings being held by candlelight in the church, as electricity was not installed until 1975.

The early days of flying at Halton. The Rothschild Estate at Halton was first used by the army for manoeuvres in 1913. When the war started Lord Rothschild offered the use of the estate to the army and the Royal Flying Corps came in 1916 and the camp was used for training recruits. In 1917 the army left, though a unit of the Australian Flying Corps joined the RFC that year. In 1918 the Air Ministry took over Halton House and it became the Officers Mess. An aircraft Apprentice scheme started in 1919 and the RAF have been training young airman there to this day.

In the Domesday book Halton was described as the lands of Lanfranc, Archbishop of Canterbury. In 1853 the manor and estate of Halton were purchased by Lionel de Rothschild, but it was not until the 1880s that his son, Alfred, built Halton House in what was called the 'free French Chateau style'. The church of St Michael, although old in origin, was entirely rebuilt in 1813, the work paid for by Sir J.D. King, then patron and Lord of the Manor.

'Aston' meant 'East-Town and 'Clinton' was added as the name of the early owners. In 1139 the manor was in the hands of William de Clinton. Centuries later Sir Anthony de Rothschild built himself Aston Clinton House, a manor later demolished except for the stable block. This view, taken around 1918, shows the London Road photographed from the Weston Turville turn. In the middle we can see W. Gates general store, later to become Cooks Store.

St Leonards was described in a survey of 1861 as a 'scattered hamlet' included in the parish of Aston Clinton. There are records of a church in the thirteenth century, largely rebuilt after the Civil War. It fell into disrepair and was restored and decorated in 1845-6. One of the oldest buildings in the village, Dundridge Cottage, seen here in the nineteenth century, has been sympathetically restored by its present owners.

Above: Wigginton High Street, showing The Brewhouse public house. In 1891 Jane Baker, a seventy-seven-year-old widow, was the 'beerhouse keeper'. It is now a private residence, restored to retain the original character.

Right: Hawridge and Cholesbury mill is situated just off Cholesbury common, on the road known as Rays Hill, and the first records of it were in 1863. It was then made of wood but when this fell into disrepair in the 1880s it was remade in stone. A cottage was added at the base of the tower and used as a grain store. Used as a mill until the First World War, it was then converted into a private dwelling and lived in until the Second World War. It was then neglected, lost its sails and was almost derelict until it was purchased and restored in the late 1960s. Still a family home today, the mill is a dominant feature in the Cholesbury countryside.

Tring Ford around 1920 with the farm in the background, now called Piggeries Pine. Tring Ford reservoir was built when the Wendover branch canal was opened and is said to be 405 feet above sea level, a trifle higher than the summit of St Paul's Cathedral.

Cooks Wharf near the Grand Union canal on the road to Cheddington. The Duke of Wellington public house is still there today. In 1891 the publican was thirty-two-year-old William Turvey, who lived with his wife, Eliza, and their two daughters, Ada and Ellen, aged six and four.